Please return on or before the date below.

D0588944

IMAGES OF CONFLICT

Dedicated to the memory of
Hansi, Hos, Dan and Anthony
and to all those who have lost their lives
in the pursuit of truth

WITHDRAWN

Rotherham College of Arts and Technology

R45110

IMAGES OF CONFLICT

THE PHOTOGRAPHS OF
HANSI KRAUSS · HOS MAINA · DAN ELDON

AP · REUTERS

THE LEARNING CENTRES
ACC No. R45110
DATE 14.9.10
CLASS 779 GAI

The publishers wish to thank everybody who assisted in the production of this book. We are particularly grateful to Danny Pope of Matchless Print Ltd. and Ilford.

First published 1993 by
Reuters Limited,
85 Fleet Street,
London
EC4.

ISBN 1-874041-11-3

This book was designed and produced by courtesy of
Camerapix,
8 Ruston Mews,
London.
 W11 1RB.

Editor: Debbie Gaiger
Production Assistant: Martha Forster
Design: Craig Dodd
Production Director: David Hewlett, First Impressions, Bratton, Wiltshire.
Colour Reproduction: D.P. Graphics, Holt, Wiltshire.
Binding: West Country Binders Ltd, Weston-super-Mare, Avon.
Paper Supply: James McNaughton Paper Ltd.

All rights reserved. No part of this publication may be reproduced, stored in a retrieval system, or transmitted in any form, or by any means, electronic, mechanical, photocopying, recording or otherwise, without permission in writing from Reuters/Associated Press.

Printed by Bath Midway Press Ltd, Holt, Wiltshire.

CONTENTS

On Monday 12 July 1993, a mob murdered four men who were working as photo-journalists in Mogadishu, Somalia. The four were separated from a convoy of media cars as they tried to photograph a United Nations helicopter assault and were attacked by angry Somalis. Those killed were Hansi Krauss (30), an Associated Press photographer from Germany; two Reuters photographers, Hos Maina (38), and Dan Eldon (22), and a Reuters sound technician, Anthony Macharia (21).

Men and women working for Reuters and The Associated Press once again had to mourn colleagues who paid the ultimate price for reporting from the rim of a volcano of inhumanity, violence and tragedy.

Hansi Krauss became the sixteenth AP reporter or photographer to die by violence in the line of duty since 1938. The death of Dan, Hos and Anthony increased Reuters' Roll of Honour to ten names since the Vietnam War.

This book shows the dedication of our dead friends to the journalistic task of reporting, their commitment to a high standard of photographic work and the compassionate touch that shines through the usually grim subjects of their photography. The portfolios left behind, especially those by Dan Eldon and Hansi Krauss, are slim; both were just at the beginning of their careers.

Unlike the works of other great photographers who died by war and violence, their photographic testaments are incomplete. The pictures in this book are just an outline of the promise of greatness that the future may have held.

Robert Capa, role model for many an aspiring news photographer, was 41 years old when he was killed by a land mine in Thai Binh, North Vietnam during the Indochina War in 1954. He began his career and first won fame photographing the seeds of war in the early 1930s. He lived through the hellfires of this century's biggest wars. His portfolio spans 25 years of the world at war.

Hansi Krauss was only 30 when he died, barely three years after he started life as a big-time photo reporter at the Berlin Wall. His work was original, but in his photographs there are intimations of what John Steinbeck saw in Capa's work 'the picture of the great heart and an overwhelming compassion.'

Larry Burrows, the dedicated and brave Life magazine photographer who carried into his war photography all the principles of compassion and excellence that characterised his pictures, was 44 years old when on 10 February 1971, his combat helicopter (with four other photographers aboard) was shot down over Laos. There were no survivors. His work shows the wide range of a man who was both a journalist and an artist. Compassionate war photography was only one part of his pre-eminent gift for composition, technical excellence, sense of beauty and strength of expression. Larry was a highly experienced photographer, and the range of his subjects was endless. British born, Larry Burrows began his career, which was to span 29 years, in London as a dark room technician.

Dan Eldon's photographs remind us of Larry Burrows. But his career lasted barely 29 months. His work shows an unusual directness. He did not dodge an issue and his photographs seem to come directly from the heart. The work of this so very young photographer expresses something rare in today's news photography: that there is not only doom and gloom, but hope and even love in the most desperate human conditions.

Hos Maina and Anthony Macharia did not have to travel far from home on their assignments. During their working lives famines and civil wars were on the doorstep of their native Kenya. Their work shows that they, too, felt responsible for making the world aware of their continent's tragedies.

The photographers whose pictures are shown in this book were not war photographers. They were professional agency photographers who did not shy away from routine jobs. They had to manage a variety of assignments from fashion shows to catastrophes, from VIP visits to soccer games. They belonged to that special breed of reporter-photographer who are forever drawn to events that challenge perceptions of the world and society, events that make history. Such events usually produce violent photographs: the turmoil of demonstrations, the brutality of war, the suffering and death of the innocent and the arrogance of power. But they can also provide a record of the good in action, of those who believe they can help.

But these photographers are not satisfied when their assignments only show us yet another famine, another civil war, another crowd of refugees, more bloodied bodies. The task these photographers set themselves is beyond mere documentation. They try to catch emotion, to peer into the hearts and minds of their subjects, so that we, the public may understand the events even better. When one simple picture says everything about the despair, the horror or the hope of a people, and such a photograph causes reaction or even compassion around the world, then is photo-journalism at its most meaningful and satisfying.

Some photographers may set out with a mission growing from a perfectly honest concern. They may want to prove that war is hell, or that mass starvation can dehumanise people. They not only report an event but become part of it.

Reporting for a news agency, as did Hansi, Hos, Dan and Anthony, is different. Like artists, news photographers may strive to do a good job while remaining outside observers, but it is hard for them to remain objective because they become deeply serious about their assignments and involved in their subjects.

Their best pictures are not accidents or strokes of luck. They are usually the result of much thought, observation and patience, plus the courage required to go where a picture must be taken. The victims of Mogadishu were not ordered to go there nor were they 'soldiers of fortune'; they had the courage to ask for assignment to Somalia.

When the news of their deaths reached the closely knit fraternity of news reporters, one reaction was heard over and over again: 'No job is worth dying for.' No doubt our friends believed that too. Any photographer who maintains that a good photograph is worth the risk of death, or worse, that he has no fear, either lies or is a danger to himself and his colleagues.

Many journalists who had to deal with similar uncontrollable situations in the past (and were lucky enough to survive) asked and analysed whether the deaths in Mogadishu could have been avoided. Did the newsmen go one step to far? There is no indication that this particular incident was more dangerous than many other events that Hansi, Hos, Dan and Anthony had covered. Newsmen and photographers that cover war and violence have to convince themselves that the death of a colleague was either caused by carelessness or that it was a tragic accident. They must convince themselves that it cannot happen to them. If a non-combatant observer, like a photographer, does not believe that, he or she cannot continue.

'There is no doubt in my mind that I, and I think most of my colleagues, would have done what they did, taken the same risk,' said one photographer, who used to work in Somalia. 'They died because fellow human beings wanted to kill them. Once confronted by their murderers they had no chance. Experience and instinct could not save them. It could have happened to any of us.'

A photographer who was working in Sarajevo when he heard about the deaths in Mogadishu was asked if he wanted to continue. He wrote to me saying, 'We all have our own reasons. Please respect those reasons and do not challenge us to justify our action. Whenever we decide to go into dangerous situations we must not believe that things will go wrong. We must be confident. That is why you must always respect anyone who says "No I will not go." We must trust our instincts.'

On the day they died in Mogadishu, our four colleagues made a judgement that the importance of the story outweighed the risks to themselves. They were trying to tell us something that they believed we needed to know. We must not forget that, as we must not forget them and all the other men and women who have died in the line of their professional duty of for their beliefs.

Horst Faas, September 1993

ANTHONY MACHARIA

Anthony Macharia on the beach in Mogadishu in June 1993

"May you live in our hearts for a thousand years
And may each year have fifty thousand days....."

Anthony Macharia was born on 5 May 1972 in the Kenyan village of Uthiru, just outside Nairobi. He was raised by his grandparents, Stanley Macharia and Salome Wanjiru, while his parents were at work. He was educated at Uthiru nursery and primary schools. Anthony graduated to Kamiti Secondary School before joining Pumwani Secondary School in Nairobi a year later. There his discipline and behaviour earned him the appointment of head prefect. His ready smile and easy manners marked him out as a natural leader, and both at school and at home he was the focus of his contemporaries. His spiritual upbringing was the charge of the Anglican St. Peter's Church, Uthiru, where he was baptized in 1978 and confirmed in 1982. At eighteen, his schooling ended and Anthony found work at Kenya Breweries. It was a job with few prospects.

He was an impressive young man with an irresistible sense of humour and clearly deserved better. I had known his family for many years so, early in 1992, I invited Anthony to join the staff of my publishing company as a picture-researcher. Despite the pressure, he displayed constant enthusiasm for his work and always had an eagle-eye for detail.

Such were his application and efforts that he transferred to the Reuters Television Africa Bureau in Nairobi after a few months to start training as a sound technician with a long-term view to him progressing to photographer or cameraman.

There he joined a close friend of his childhood, Patrick Muiruri, and became a formidable addition to the camera crew. Anthony was modest and unassuming, always cheerful and no load was too great for him, nor any task too menial. He was eager to help in every way and was clearly cut out for the job and its challenges. Indeed, we marked him down for a great future in the intense competition of international television news.

Soundmen are the third member of any television camera crew, sharing the risk equally with correspondent and cameraman, but rarely with any public recognition. During the years many have died in action alongside their camera colleagues — tied by the umbilical cord of the recording equipment. Anthony had no concept of fear and his new responsibilities were characterised by an increasing degree of self-confidence and an intense enthusiasm for work. The greater the challenge, the greater Anthony's response.

His smiling face each morning brought a fresh sparkle to our Nairobi office. He was always willing to help his friends and colleagues in the office with any aspect of the work when he was not travelling on assignment. His first assignments were with Patrick in Kenya but he was soon travelling outside the country. Anthony first travelled to Somalia early in 1993.

Two months later he returned to Mogadishu fearless in the face of the aggressive mobs, always ready to joke and laugh with international news colleagues. Anthony was a tremendous colleague and a fine friend, a strength to lean on during the dangerous hours — virtues he displayed under fire in the frontline. His death on 12 July 1993 is a tragedy for his family and a loss for many. He will always be missed and his memory treasured by his friends and colleagues in the world of international television news.

Mohamed Amin, September 1993

HANSI KRAUSS

Hansi Krauss on assignment in Mogadishu, Somalia 9 July 1993.

It did not take Hansi Krauss, who always climbed above the crowds, long to win some of the toughest and most dangerous assignments offered to an Associated Press photographer. The fearless, upbeat, friendly young man, was usually first on the scene with his trademark baseball cap worn backwards. He was born Hansjoerg Krauss on 29 April 1963. Nicknamed Hansi, he was the second son of a local physician and grew up in the small Black Forest town of Trossingen in south-west Germany.

His irrepressible energy and enthusiasm were evident from an early age. During his days at high school he played the drums and enjoyed the dangerous sports of ski-jumping and rock-climbing, funding these hobbies with a newspaper round. Despite these flamboyant interests, Hansi was always a careful and sensitive person.

The demolition of the Trossingen ski-jump platform brought Hansi into photography. He staked out the rotting construction for days until he was finally chased away by the contractor. During this time he photographed every nut and bolt, creating a photographic essay which told the story of its demise.

After graduating from Trossingen High School in 1983, and briefly flirting with a career in medicine, Hansi's thirst for adventure and challenge led him to the trails and mountains of Norway, and in 1985 onto the peaks of the Yosemite National Park and on a canoeing expedition down the Yukon River.

Having returned to Germany, Hansi was badly injured in a car accident and was forced to suspend his travelling ambitions for a year while recuperating. He joined Associated Press in 1989 when Berlin became the focus of the world's attention. He was always fearless and his determination is remembered by his close friends in the business. He was easily found in a crowd of thousands — usually impossibly perched on a ledge or in a tree trying to get the best pictures. Berlin was his first major story and Hansi was driven by the satisfaction of seeing his pictures on the front pages. He readily accepted the risks which accompany working in such chaotic and unpredictable situations. More than once he was beaten up covering riots when Berlin's right and left-wing extremists took to the streets. Hansi complained more about his broken camera gear than about his bruised and swollen face. He had become the classic street photographer, who excelled in turbulent conditions.

His devotion towards his job and his desire to be at the centre of the action led Hansi to volunteer to travel to Sarajevo in September 1992 and again in January 1993. He is remembered there as a man who never lost his sense of humour and who never allowed danger to compromise his story.

When the United States, followed by the United Nations, intervened in the troubles of Somalia, Hansi was eager to cover the first-ever deployment of German UN troops. In June 1993, he was given permission to go and departed with his characteristic enthusiasm.

Tragically, Hansi died on 12 July at the hands of an angry Somali mob in Mogadishu, the day after he had transmitted a joyful photograph of young Somali orphans — a picture of hope from one of the world's most desperate places.

Hansi is remembered around the world by colleagues, loved ones and friends for his strength and humanity. His intense and extraordinary life was much too short, but his images will stand as his autobiography.

Andreas Kuther, September 1993.

Above: West Berlin 27 February 1990 — A girl climbs over the Berlin Wall from East to West in front of the Brandenburg Gate. The East Germans started dismantling this part of the wall the night before. Unhindered passage was possible by the end of March.

Opposite top: West Berlin 19 February 1990 — A couple enters East Berlin close to West Berlin's Reichstag building through a hole in the Berlin Wall.

Opposite: West Berlin 14 January 1990 — Children enjoy a moment of play in the holes in the Berlin Wall near the Brandenburg Gate. The holes were made by tourists from all over the world, who took parts of the wall as souvenirs.

Above: Bosnia Herzegovina 15 February 1993 — Relatives mourn and pray at the grave of a civilian in Sarajevo's Lion cemetery. Since all trees in the cemetery of the besieged city were cut for firewood, the place has become exposed to sniper fire, forcing mourners to visit early in the morning to reduce the risk of being shot.

Opposite: Bosnia Herzegovina 26 January 1993 — A brother and sister mourn over the grave of their father during funeral services at the snow-covered Lion cemetery in Sarajevo. Their father was killed during shelling of Sarajevo by Serbian forces.

Above: Bosnia Herzegovina February 1993 — Mourners at the grave of a loved one.

Opposite: Bosnia Herzegovina 20 February 1993 — Bosnian soldiers stand next to the grave of a fallen comrade, waiting to fire a volley at Sarajevo's military cemetery.

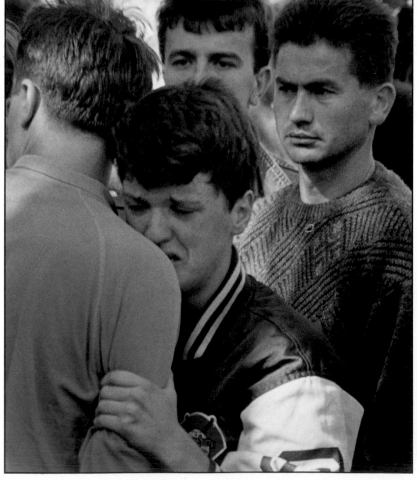

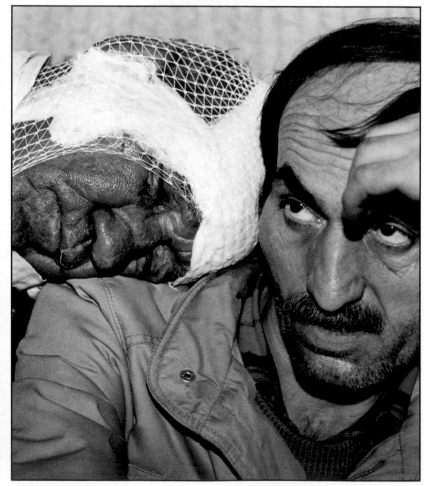

Above: Bosnia Herzegovina 15 September 1992 — Bosnian refugees who fled fighting are seen in Kiseljak, a town 18 miles north-west of Sarajevo. The refugees were making their way back from Zagreb to their home town in Tuzla.

Opposite top left: Bosnia Herzegovina 24 January 1993 — A father and son weep over the death of a family member.

Opposite top right: Bosnia Herzegovina 24 January 1993 — A man and his son cry over the death of their wife and mother in Sarajevo. The woman was killed while sitting in her living-room when a shell hit the apartment building.

Opposite left: Bosnia Herzegovina 16 September 1992 — Bosnian militiamen weep as one of their fellow soldiers is buried at Sarajevo's Lion cemetery.

Opposite right: Bosnia Herzegovina 20 September 1992 — The burned face of an old man injured during a mortar attack near his home.

Above: Bosnia Herzegovina 30 January 1993 — Passers-by help injured people lying in the street in front of the Bosnian Presidency after a shell hit the crowded street. One person was killed and eight others wounded.

Opposite: Bosnia Herzegovina 30 January 1993 — A seriously wounded Bosnian militiaman is carried out of a truck at the former military hospital in Sarajevo. The man, who was fighting in the western Sarajevo suburb of Stup, died shortly after reaching the hospital.

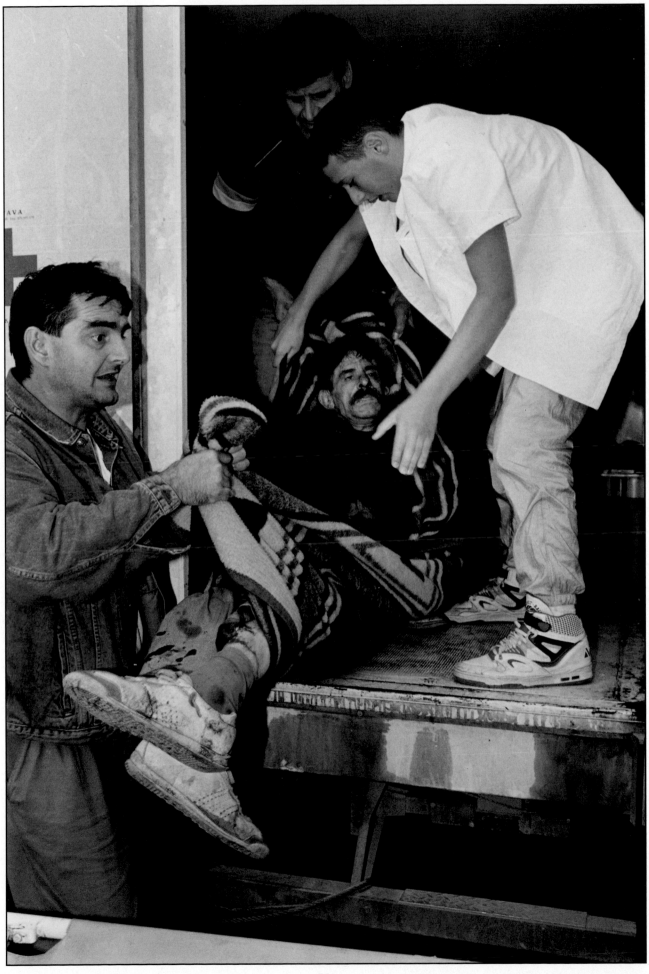

Above: Bosnia Herzegovina 9 February 1993 — In the old section of Sarajevo a Bosnian woman carries firewood on her back for heating and cooking. The wood was cut out of an abandoned house that was hit by artillery fire a few days before.

Above: Bosnia Herzegovina 19 September 1992 — A man walks by a
shattered storefront. As the days grew shorter in Sarajevo, the municipal
authorities attempted to replace broken windows in the besieged city before
winter set in.

Above: Bosnia Herzegovina 26 January 1993 — A Bosnian man pushes his wheelbarrow loaded with supplies across an intersection frequently fired upon by snipers near the Milijacka river in Sarajevo.

Opposite top: Berlin 1 May 1990 — Berlin police arrest a demonstrator during riots in the district of Kreuzberg. Hundreds of masked youths threw stones and fire bombs against police.

Opposite: Bosnia Herzegovina 28 January 1993 — A woman showing a photograph of her son protests and blocks the street with her husband and other Sarajevans in front of the Bosnian Presidency. They accused the Bosnian military of having arrested 170 Bosnian soldiers who switched to the Croatian side.

Above: Mogadishu 11 July 1993 — Luul Mohamud is surrounded by orphans in a former Mogadishu school which she converted into the Restore Hope Orphanage. This became a safe haven for more than 1,000 orphans under the age of ten.

Above: Mogadishu 28 June 1993 — Eager Somalis crowd around
food supplies in a feeding centre. As food distribution continued, the
death tolls came down.

Above: Mogadishu 30 June 1993 — Young boy holds his hands up as he passes through a United Nations checkpoint.

Opposite: Mogadishu 25 June 1993 — A boy says hello to a soldier. Somali children have long become accustomed to the fighting and a military presence in the capital.

Above: Mogadishu 23 June 1993 — Somali children beg for sweets from a
United Nations soldier.

Above: Mogadishu 23 June 1993 — Somali children share a drink with a
United Nations soldier at a Mogadishu checkpoint.

Above: Mogadishu 9 July 1993 — A Somali crowd demonstrates in favour
of warlord Mohamed Farah Aideed.

Opposite: Mogadishu 5 July 1993 — A water carrier plods through the rain-
swept streets of Mogadishu.

HOS MAINA

Hos Maina on assignment in Mogadishu, Somalia July 1993.

"How sleep the brave, who sink to rest,
By all their country's wishes blest."
William Collins

Hos Maina was one of the finest individuals I have ever had the pleasure of knowing and the privilege of working alongside. He was an exceptionally brave man. Not in the reckless manner of some international photographers, but in a far deeper, more meaningful way.

Hos nearly died in a car crash a little over three years ago. A local Catholic priest read the last rites, but Hos fought back from the precipice of death, spurred on by the thought of his young family, to resume work a few months later.

But it was to be a long, hard — and often thankless — road back. Permanent injuries often left him depressed and frustrated that a job once so easy had become difficult.

But never once did he think of quitting, only of ways to accelerate his return to peak performance. He spent hours learning new techniques to overcome the disability of a half-paralysed right hand and examining ways to make the business of transmitting photographs easier for him to manage.

It is a dreadful irony that by the time of his death he was shooting his best photographs for several years. During those last terrifying weeks in Mogadishu, he had won front pages on newspapers across the world and much praise from the London picture desk. He was immensely proud to be back at the top of his profession. In that way, at least, he died a happy man.

He loved news photography with a passion — an emotion only truly understood by other news photographers. Like many of the best journalists, he also loved people and had a great appetite and zest for life.

Like many of my colleagues, I travelled widely with Hos — usually to places of great despair. Despite the many human tragedies we encountered along the way, I have only fond memories of those days. There were always many jokes, a lot of laughter and a few tears. But Hos had a great eye for finding that small piece of joy among the endless misery which elevated his best photographs to something higher than simple news.

Hos, who met his own death in such violent circumstances, was an extremely gentle man. He had few bad words for anyone and was generous with both his knowledge and his time. Many young Kenyans wishing to emulate him, would visit the office for advice and tips. Hos had time for them all.

It is a tribute to his work and his character that since his death the Nairobi bureau has been inundated with messages of condolence from all over the world, most of which mention his kindness and his patience.

Hos Maina's death has left a great void in many lives, not just for his friends and workmates but for his wife Lucy and their three children.

All those who worked with him miss him far more as a friend than a colleague.

Jonathan Clayton, September 1993

35

Above: Mogadishu 21 June 1993 — Two Somali women carry their rations from a distribution centre, while a United Nations peace-keeping soldier keeps guard in his tank. The relief food was distributed following UN attacks on Somali warlord Mohamed Farah Aideed's weapons dumps.

Opposite top: Mogadishu 15 June 1993 — Supporters of Aideed cheer their leader at a rally. The United Nations launched three air strikes that week, blasting weapons and ammunition dumps in Mogadishu following the deaths of twenty-four Pakistani peace-keepers in an ambush on 5 June.

Opposite: Mogadishu 15 June 1993 — Somali warlord Mohamed Farah Aideed addresses a rally of supporters.

Above: Mogadishu 5 June 1993 — United Nations soldiers attempt to control
Somali women as they wait to receive food relief.

Above: Mogadishu 5 June 1993 — A food distribution centre guarded by
Pakistani soldiers.

Above: Mogadishu 22 June 1993 — Somalis walking from the market pass a
United Nations peace-keeper's machine gun nest. Security increased after UN
attacks on Aideed's ammunition dumps.

Above: Mogadishu 17 June 1993 — A United Nations soldier takes cover while
UN troops storm Mohamed Farah Aideed's residence in Mogadishu.

Above: Mogadishu 18 June 1993 — Relatives carry the body of a woman killed in a helicopter attack when the United Nations was engaged in a seven-hour fight with militia loyal to Somali warlord Mohamed Farah Aideed.

Above: Mogadishu 5 June 1993 — Somalis run for cover during sniper fire.

Above: Mogadishu 10 June 1993 — A food distribution centre guarded by
Pakistani soldiers, part of the United Nations peace-keeping force in Somalia..

Above: Southern Sudan March 1993 — Victims of warring factions in Sudan
wait for food distribution.

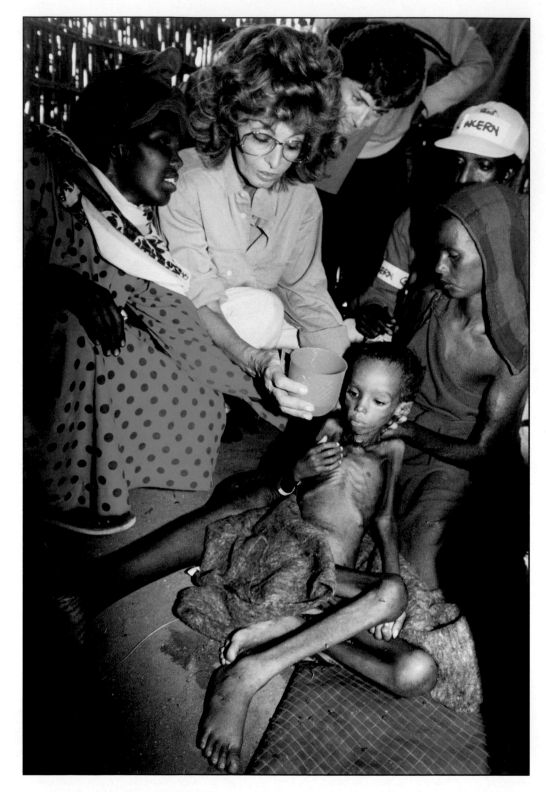

Above: Somalia 23 November 1992 — Sophia Loren feeds starving child
during a mercy mission to the famine-stricken country.

Opposite: Mogadishu 10 February 1993 — A small boy at a food distribution
centre wanders through the recently delivered sacks of grain.

Above: Mogadishu 10 December 1992 — Somalis watch as United States army troops arrive in Mogadishu as part of Operation Restore Hope.

Opposite: Mogadishu 23 November 1992 — A young famine victim roams among the debris that litters Mogadishu. Thousands died in Somalia from famine and other diseases. Many will never recover from the shock induced by the scenes of devastation they have experienced.

DAN ELDON

Above: Somalia December 1992 — Dan Eldon with a crowd of smiling Somali youngsters.

"For he was likely, had he been put on, to have proved most royally" — Hamlet

Somalia was Dan Eldon's first and, most cruelly, his only assignment for Reuters. More than any other journalist covering that wretched country he made it his story. For the dozens of special correspondents that poured into the country, to visit Mogadishu without meeting Dan was unthinkable — such was the legend he became in his tragically short career. His familiarity with the city and knowledge of the local scene earned him the nickname "Mayor of Mogadishu". He was equally at ease strolling through Mogadishu's notorious Sakhara market, playing with street kids, sipping "shahi" with gunmen, or dining with UN troop commanders.

Dan's reputation as a photographer was made the same way his short life ended — bringing Somalia's agony to the attention of the world. He was one of the first photographers to go to the famine areas last summer and helped put "the land God forgot" on the world agenda.

He began making more and more trips into Somalia and his work became better and better. He was eager to learn and absorbed something from every one of several more experienced photographers who flocked to cover first the famine and then the US intervention last December to protect food conveys from marauding gunmen.

As his photography matured, he grew as an individual. In the space of little more than nine months, Dan Eldon moved from being an enthusiastic young man with lots of raw talent to being a true professional. It was a measure of his development and a tribute to his skill, that when Somalia again made the headlines in June, there was no question of Reuters head office sending in an outsider. By now, it was Dan's story and he could do it alone. He did and won magnificent play in the process, including double-page spreads in *Time* and *Newsweek*.

Dan took his success modestly and won many friends with an impish sense of humour and disarming honesty. He had many projects in mind and was never inactive for long. He lightened many evening hours in the Reuters Mogadishu house with spoof videos of his colleagues and hungrily learned editing and sound techniques from visiting television journalists. Above all else, it was always fun working and being with Dan.

He was the son of an American mother and English father who moved to Nairobi when he was seven years old. From an early age he was involved in charitable activities, often raising money for projects he considered important. In 1989 he founded Student Transport Aid and, together with 14 other university friends, raised US$25,000. Dan led the group from Nairobi to Malawi, where they donated a Land Cruiser, money for two wells, and vital supplies to a settlement of refugees from Mozambique. He spent most of his life in Kenya and was at ease in Africa in a way that few whites not born on this beguiling continent ever manage. He had a profound respect for and deep understanding of its people and customs which translated through his work.

It was a love and knowledge of Africa that enabled him to capture moments of beauty and hope amid the most appalling suffering. This gave many of his photographs that little extra spin which ensured their success. He occasionally spoke of returning to University in California to complete his studies, but few of us who witnessed the relish with which he attacked his work believed he could give it up.

He had sensed it was time to leave Mogadishu and it is a particularly cruel twist of fate that he met his death on the day his replacement arrived to take over. But it was typical he should have gone out one last time for he would never miss an opportunity whilst still in town.

Those of us who worked closely with Dan miss him greatly, but equally we are deeply proud that we were able to share a little bit of the stage on which he shone so brightly.

Jonathan Clayton, September 1993

Above: Mogadishu 12 April 1993 — Thousands of Somali Bantus demonstrate outside the stadium in Mogadishu in support of peace and to show their unified political power. The Bantu minority was one of the Somali groups worst hit by looting and crop raiding during the civil war. Hundreds of thousands of Bantus starved to death during the war.

Opposite top: Mogadishu 8 June 1993 — A group of Somali youths at a rally in Mogadishu. They waved pictures of their leader, fugitive warlord Mohamed Farah Aideed, wanted by the United Nations for his alleged involvement in the incident where Pakistani peace-keeping soldiers were ambushed by Somali gunmen.

Opposite: Mogadishu 19 June 1993 — Anti-American demonstrators in support of Mohamed Farah Aideed in Mogadishu. Some of the protesters wave pictures of Aideed and Saddam Hussein, claiming their Muslim brotherhood in the fight against America.

Top: Mogadishu 6 July 1993 — An American soldier befriends a Somali boy
in the war-torn capital of Somalia.

Above: Mogadishu 6 July 1993 — Even the children are searched.

Opposite: Mogadishu 15 February 1993 — In a land ruled by the gun,
children use broken guns as toys.

Above: Mogadishu 12 February 1993 — A smiling Somali girl runs through a flooded store — a rare moment of joy in a country ravaged by war, famine and strife.

Above: Mogadishu 20 January 1993 — US soldier gives a drink to a young Somali boy.
In the early days of the American intervention foreign troops were welcomed by
Somalis, but the honeymoon turned sour soon after control was handed over from US
to United Nations command on 4 May 1993.

Above: Mogadishu 8 March 1993 — A Somali girl holds a rifle for a guard while he prays in a compound. Somali women have seldom been active participants in the clan clashes, but thousands have been wounded by stray bullets, looting incidents and rape.

Opposite: Mogadishu 11 July 1993 — Guns and bikinis — a startling contrast between the chaos of civil war. Sunday is beach day for the United Nations forces in Somalia who face mortar attacks daily.

Above: Mogadishu 7 April 1993 — US marines patrol Mogadishu's gutted museum. All of the artefacts and exhibits, as well as the roof, have been looted.

Opposite: Mogadishu 10 January 1993 — US soldier on patrol in Mogadishu's central Catholic Cathedral, reportedly the largest in Africa. It is situated close to the "green line" dividing the city's two main rival clans and is a notorious hiding place for snipers and bandits.

Above: Mogadishu 3 April 1993 — US Marine Lance Corporal Harold Clawson
from Kentucky stands guard beside a shell-ravaged mosque in the area which
used to be Mogadishu's business district.

Above: Mogadishu 9 March 1993 — A US Marine stands alert minutes after his squad
received sniper fire near Mogadishu's main market. Somali children are so used to the
sound of gunfire that they jokingly call it "Somali music".

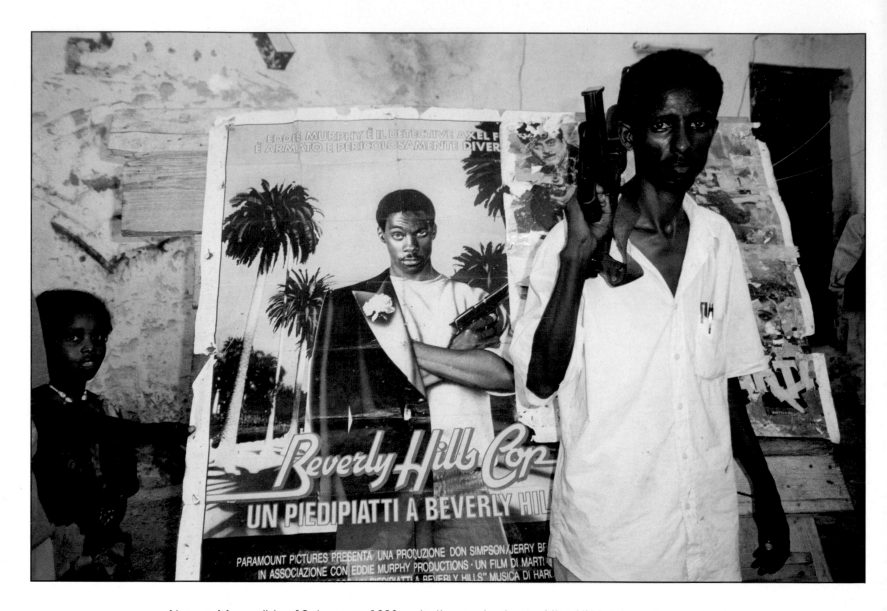

Above: Mogadishu 12 January 1993 — In the early days of the UN intervention, a short-lived peace saw the re-opening of local cinemas. Somali youths identified with gun-toting American cops.

Opposite top: Mogadishu 14 February 1993 — A US Marine points a pistol at a Somali youth after seizing it from the 15-year-old boy near Mogadishu's "green line".

Opposite: Mogadishu 6 March 1993 — A Somali walks past a cinema where a sign tells patrons it is forbidden to carry weapons inside the theatre. The Stars and Stripes typeface on the wall became very popular after the arrival of the Americans in December 1992.

Above: Mogadishu 15 February 1993 — A bound suspected gunman picked up during a routine search for weapons kneels on waste ground on the edge of the capital. Such patrols became more infrequent as United Nations forces relied more on airpower.

Above: Mogadishu 12 February 1993 — US soldier guards a suspected Somali gunman. United Nations soldiers first went to Somalia to protect food supplies from marauding groups of gunmen, but their tactics became increasingly tough as they found themselves locked into a guerrilla war.

Opposite: Mogadishu 18 December 1992 — A Somali gunman guards a feeding centre in Baidoa.
Prior to the intervention by US troops, gangsters profited from looting and extortion.

Above: Mogadishu 18 December 1992 — An old man mourns the death of his wife and four of
their children.

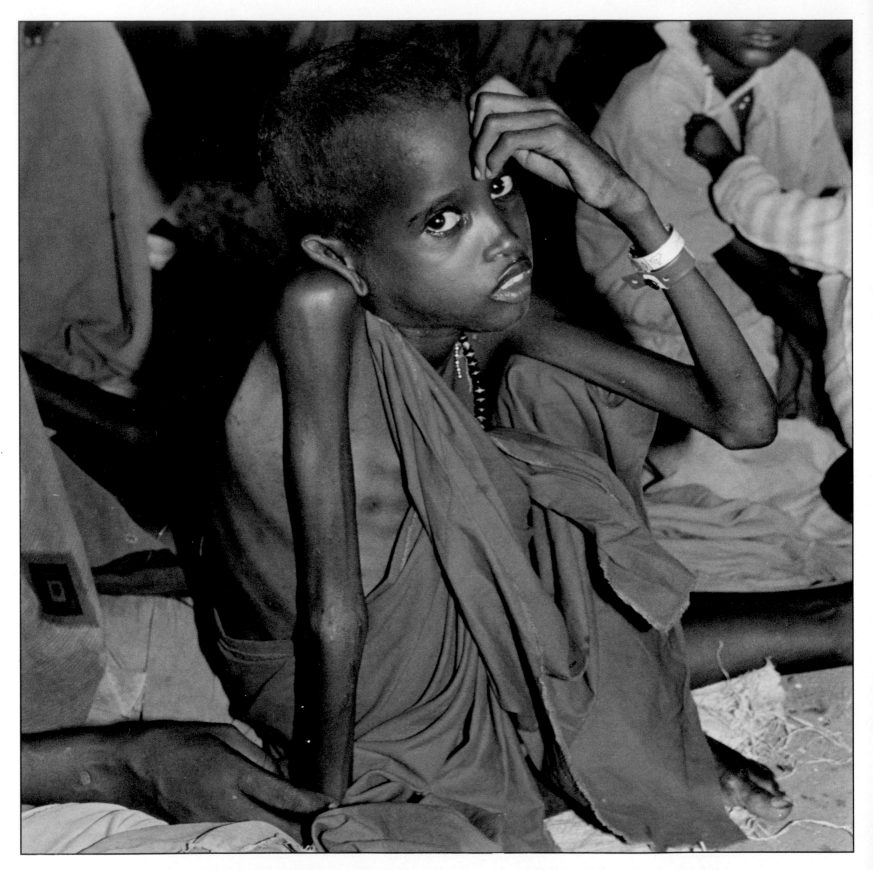

Above: Mogadishu 18 December 1992 — A starving Somali child stares blankly ahead.

Opposite: Mogadishu 20 December 1992 — Thousands of children are unlikely to ever recover from the shock induced by the terrible scenes of carnage they have witnessed.

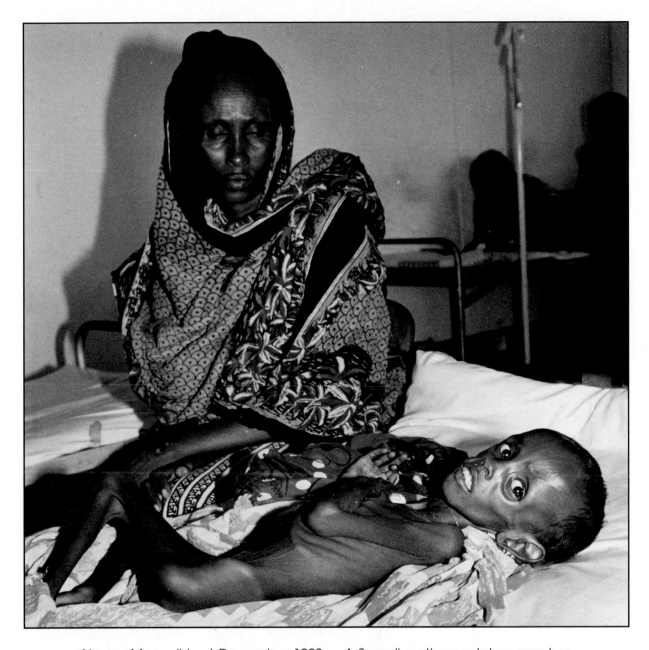

Above: Mogadishu 6 December 1992 — A Somali mother watches over her dying child in Mogadishu's Benadir hospital. Hundreds of thousands of children have died in Somalia's war of famine.

Opposite: Mogadishu 15 December 1992 — More famine victims await death. Starving Somalis, their crops and homes destroyed in fighting between rival clans, walked miles to the nearest town in search of food. Many died on the way. Other survived the journey, but were too weak to hang onto life.

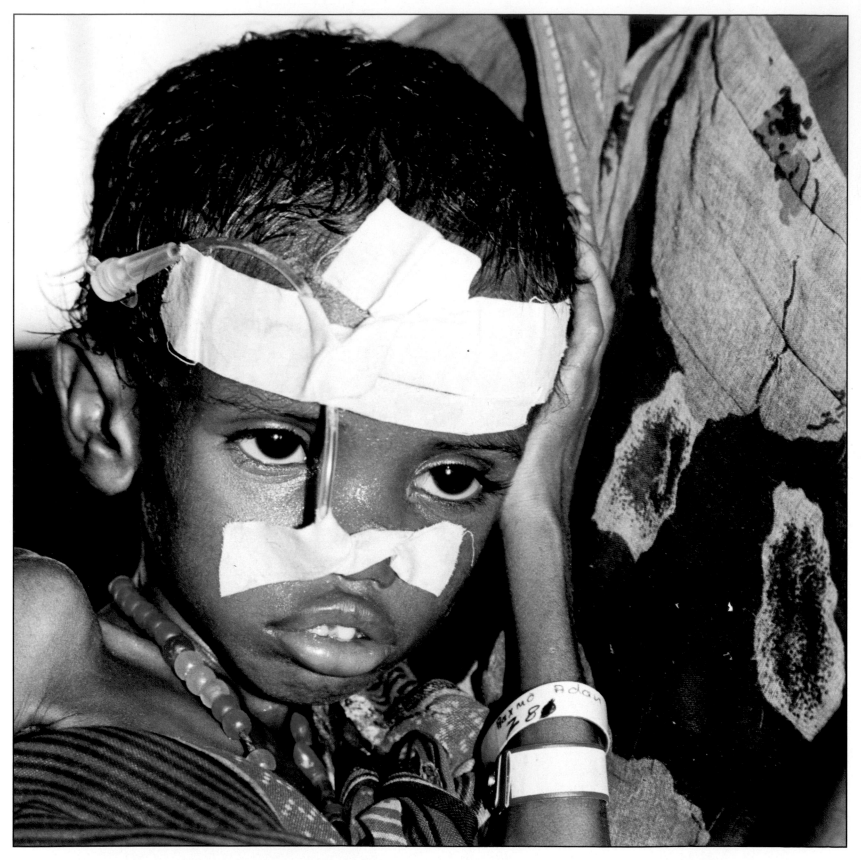

Above: Mogadishu 3 December 1992 — A starving child receives life-saving aid in a hospital in advance of the US led relief intervention in Somalia.

Opposite: Mogadishu 7 December 1992 — A malnourished Somali child waits for a cup of gruel.

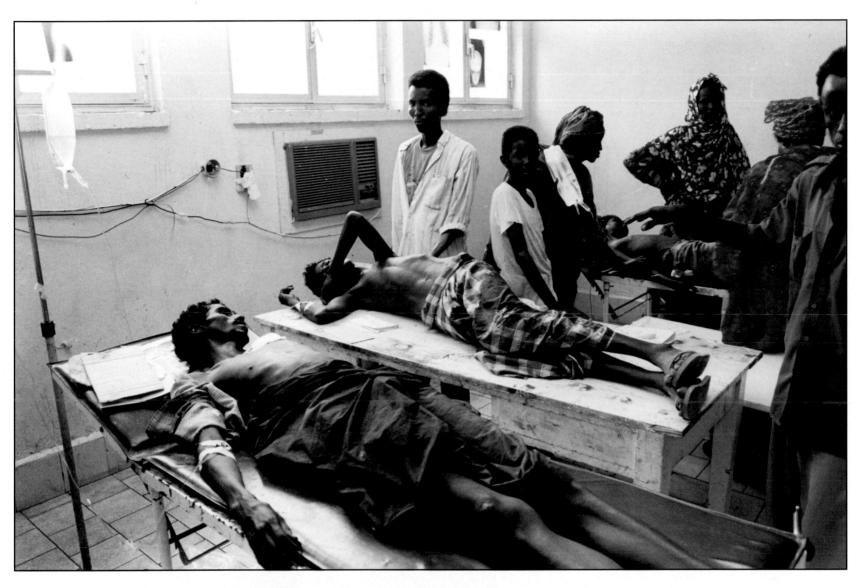

Above: Mogadishu 13 June 1993 — Wounded Somalis are treated for gunshot wounds at a hospital in Mogadishu. They were shot by United Nations Pakistani peace-keeping troops in an incident where a demonstration turned bloody.

Opposite top: Mogadishu 13 June 1993 — Somali children flee from US Army Cobra assault helicopters.

Opposite: Mogadishu 12 June 1993 — US army helicopters hovering over Somali warlord Mohamed Farah Aideed's destroyed tanks after a UN strike on ammunition stores.

Above: Mogadishu 8 June 1993 — UN Pakistani troops load the coffins of their twenty-four fallen comrades who were killed during clashes with Somali gunmen loyal to Mohamed Farah Aideed.

Opposite top: Mogadishu 18 June 1993 — US Marines rush from a helicopter with another vicitim of a Somali sniper's bullet. UN troops, locked in an increasingly ugly guerrilla war with gunmen loyal to Aideed, often come under attack from snipers hiding in the city's bombed out buildings.

Opposite: Mogadishu 18 June 1993 — A young Somali boy helps his family move to a safe neighbourhood in Mogadishu fearing further air strikes by the United Nations.